I'm Deaf Too

12 DEAF AMERICANS

Published by the
National Association of the Deaf
814 Thayer Avenue
Silver Spring, Maryland

Frank Bowe

Martin Sternberg

Copyright © 1973 Frank G. Bowe and Martin L.A. Sternberg
All Rights Reserved
ISBN: 0-913072-06-0
Library of Congress Catalog Number: 73-79377
Printed in the United States of America
Published By
The National Association of the Deaf
814 Thayer Avenue
Silver Spring, Maryland 20910
2nd Printing 1988

Thank you

We are in debt to many people.

To Norm Tully, who first suggested that the book be written; to Jess Smith for his continuing support of the original *Deaf American* interviews and for permission to edit these selected interviews for inclusion in the book; to Fred Schreiber and the National Association of the Deaf for publishing it; to Jerome Schein, Director of the New York University Deafness Research & Training Center for his support; to Glenn Lloyd, for his editorial expertise; to Janet Winslow and Shelley Shackleford for their very able assistance in preparing the manuscript; to Frank Turk for his inspiring Foreword; to the deaf subjects who really wrote the book; and finally to the deaf community, whose interest made it all possible.

Frank G. Bowe
Martin L. A. Sternberg

New York, February 1, 1973

Contents

Foreword by Frank Turk vii

Introduction 1

Miss Deaf America ANN BILLINGTON 2

The Deaf Actor and Director BERNARD BRAGG 8

Deaf People and TTY's LEE BRODY 12

Chance and Choice EDWARD CARNEY 16

To Be Black and Deaf ERNEST HAIRSTON 20

Dentistry and the Clergy EDWIN NIES 24

The Deaf Woman NANCY RARUS 28

The Deaf Man at Work BEN SCHOWE 34

The Deaf Counselor LARRY STEWART 38

The Deaf Man and Insurance FRANK SULLIVAN 44

Deaf People and Television JANE WILK 50

Wrestling in Arkansas NATHAN ZIMBLE 54

Foreword
by Frank Turk

This manual is intended largely to serve as an around-the-clock helper in our academic programs for the deaf throughout the United States of America. It has been carefully planned to make available a practical and inspirational reading resource for deaf children presently in attendance at schools. Its chief objective is to get all school-age deaf children motivated to do their very best at all times *on their own* in developing *their own* adult structures. It affords an opportunity for young deaf people to learn from the mistakes and triumphs of successful deaf adults on a continuing basis—the deaf adults who were what the youngsters are; who felt the way they feel, and who saw things the way they see them. Inspirational guidance in the critical lessons of life is the point of emphasis here, guidance which transcends the theoretical.

Every deaf youngster needs help today just to lead a normal life. A commencement speaker at Gallaudet College stated that "we are in the midst of a knowledge explosion. We all have to run just to stay where we are." Nowhere in this country can you find a successful deaf man who achieved his success without the help of his fellow beings. The average deaf person performs below the level of his ability unless he is encouraged to undertake projects larger than he feels he can handle. He is constantly struggling with himself and needs inspiring guidance to make the struggle effective. The inspiration that he gains from people who are important to him is of incalculable assistance here—something that can serve as an omnipresent aid to his becoming all that he is meant to be.

This manual is a synthesis of the successes and failures of some of the most successful deaf adults in America—those who are yesterday's deaf children grown-up and who now possess the sophistication so necessary to conquer the many difficult learning and becoming situations for and with today's deaf youth.

Of all educational tools in the present era of innovations and technological advances, there is nothing more effective and influential than inspirational guidance in the life of a young deaf learner who is struggling at all times to close the gap between his present and potential levels of the potential contributions inherent in the realm of inspirational guidance: Years ago at the Minnesota School for the Deaf while I was dance: Years ago at the Minnesota School for the Deaf while I was waiting, along with several other miscreants, to be reprimanded for some forgotten misdeed, a hearing houseparent came in and placed a piece of paper listing his complaints on the lectern. He was completely disgusted with us, and although he was fully justified in feeling thus, he made it known to us in such a way that we resented his very presence. As his anger increased, we countered with a rebellious attitude, making stealthy comments to one another: "Aw, that aint so," "He makes up the story," "He thinks we are a bunch of blockheads," and "We are not that bad." After his talk, he had a discussion with a deaf houseparent during which he showed the latter his written list of complaints. When the deaf houseparent took the stage with the self-same list, our immediate opinion of him, unknowing that he had the same list, was this: "He is a good man and always tries to help us. It is a shame that we have let him down." We were psychologically responsive and receptive to his scoldings, even though he covered the same things that the other man did. Our responses were "I am ashamed of myself," "He is right," "He wants to help us," and "We are wrong. We gotta improve ourselves." The same complaints, the same scolding, but in an understanding way and from someone we could identify ourselves with—it made all the difference in the world!

Opportunities for informal contacts with outstanding deaf youngsters and adults on a continuing basis should be utilized as an integral part of any school curriculum. This practice can serve as a fine compensation for the loss of sound experiences—something that has not been tried on a continuing basis and perhaps something the absence of which, more than anything else, has been indirectly responsible for the failure of deaf citizens to compete on equal terms with their hearing contemporaries.

Thank you, Frank Bowe and Martin L. A. Sternberg, for an extremely valuable contribution. It is hoped that the ideas and suggestions contained in the manual will be utilized, maintained, and expanded by all concerned in the same serious spirit with which they were brought together. They can, in a sense, serve much as the guiding force we so deeply need in our efforts to bring about the "day of awakening" for all the deaf.

Frank R. Turk, Director
Youth Relations Program at Gallaudet College
Junior NAD

Introduction

Growing up deaf, we often wondered how our lives would be affected by the handicap. We asked questions about deaf adults, their jobs, their lives.

We sought answers in vain.

Unfortunately, the educational policy then was to isolate deaf children from deaf adults. We lacked models to pattern ourselves after, career goals to strive for, heroes.

This book was written to provide today's deaf youth with some answers. As the book developed, we realized that parents of deaf children and professionals in the field might have some of the same questions.

This is a book of questions and answers. We talked with successful deaf adults about their lives. They told us about their childhoods, their dreams, their daily lives, what deafness means to them.

What they had to say could fill a book—and has.

F.B.
M.S.

Miss Deaf America
Ann Billington

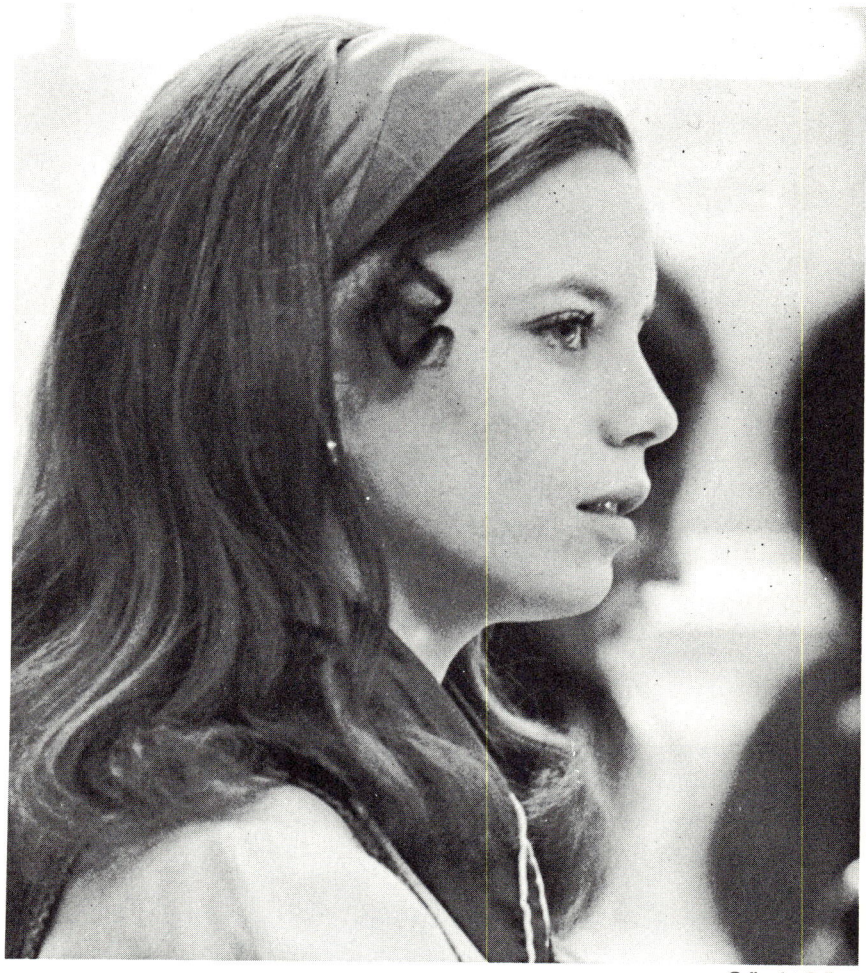

Gallaudet College

ANN BILLINGTON was born in Tulsa, Oklahoma. She attended Central Institute for the Deaf in St. Louis, transferring to a private hearing school in her home town at the age of nine. In September, 1970 Ann enrolled as a freshman at Gallaudet. She was named Miss Deaf America on July 6, 1972.

Ann, how did you feel when you were crowned Miss Deaf America?

I was excited and a bit scared. I knew it meant a lot of responsibility. Most of all, I was really happy to be able to represent deaf people. I've always had a strong urge to prove what deaf people can do.

Is that why you entered the competition?

Actually, I did not plan on entering the contest at Gallaudet, much less the Miss Deaf America Pageant. What happened is that the Editor-in-Chief of the Gallaudet newspaper, the *Buff & Blue*, asked me if I would be interested in representing the paper at the Miss Gallaudet Pageant. I accepted because I thought it would be a good experience and I wanted to enjoy the opportunity.

One week before the pageant, I still didn't know what talent category I would enter! My father, who is a musician, sent me a song called "Hey, Look Me Over." He searched 48 hours to find that song. I danced "The Sailor's Hornpipe" while I sang the song.

The Gallaudet pageant was held January 27 and 28, 1972. Each class at Gallaudet and each organization on campus was represented by a contestant. We went through the first round on January 27. The top ten girls performed again the next day. We had cocktail dress, talent and evening gown competitions.

Then it was narrowed down to five finalists. Each of us had to answer a question. I was asked: "Do you think your deafness will hinder your interest in the fashion world and why?"

I answered: "No, because I've had some experience with fashion and modeling and I can prove, as a deaf person, that I am able to do anything expected of me. All you have to do is just to model clothes and walk down the runway. You don't need to hear to model. If they won't accept me, I will fight for it, and I will do it!" That statement won me the title of Miss Gallaudet. I received an all expense-paid trip to Miami Beach, Florida, for the National Association of the Deaf convention where the Miss Deaf America Pageant was to be held.

What happened at Miami Beach?

There were only five of us in the Pageant because it was the first one in the NAD's history. We went through the same procedure: cocktail dress, talent and evening gown. I did the same song. Finally came the question: "What are your plans for your career?"

My answer was: "My plans after I graduate from Gallaudet are to go to a fashion college in Dallas, Texas, for one year to study how to buy and sell clothes and to design clothes and also to model part-time. But I also want to help the deaf with any problems. I also feel that God will have a lot of responsibilities for me to do the work for Him and for all you deaf people. I know it takes a lot of courage to do the work, but I am willing to face all the challenges in the world."

What is it like being Miss Deaf America?

I'm still not used to the idea that I actually am Miss Deaf America. Miss Deaf America has a lot of invitations to attend state conventions of deaf organizations to show her winning talent and to give speeches. Last semester I was honored to sit at the head table at the banquet of the Mayor's Committee on Employment of the Handicapped. I will attend some meetings of hearing clubs to represent deaf people.

Next summer I'll be going to Colorado for the state NAD chapter convention. I have received a scholarship to attend the summer workshop with the National Theatre of the Deaf in Waterford, Connecticut. I will also be involved in one of the Inauguration Events for President Nixon.

Miss Deaf America has a national role to play. She should be an asset to deaf people everywhere. The Miss Deaf America Pageant also offers young deaf people the opportunity to develop their poise, self-confidence, talent and personality. It will help them become aware of their potentials and help them reach for ever greater heights.

Do you enjoy being a student at Gallaudet College?

Oh, yes. I am a Junior majoring in English, with a minor in fashion. I have also been a member of the Modern Dance Club, the *Buff & Blue,* the Student Assembly of the Student Body Government, and the cheerleaders. My hobbies are dancing, swimming, modeling, sewing, reading, traveling, meeting people and I am a dog lover. I love animals extremely, except for snakes!

Would you like to say anything to the deaf youth of America?

I would encourage deaf youth to start their education as early as possible and to keep it up through college. We deaf should have as much education as we can.

I would also encourage deaf youth to participate in many different activities that would help them work better with hearing people. Of course, we're very shy, but we must learn to overcome this shyness. I happen to be a very shy person, but I'll never show it. Forcing myself to go out and meet all kinds of people has helped me to develop more courage and self-confidence. I also want to encourage deaf girls to enter a beauty pageant to learn what it is like to compete with other girls. This is a good opportunity to make new friends and to develop your personality.

I think patience is very important. Without patience, one might become frustrated and deeply hurt. But with patience, one will be blessed. One must not be selfish and try to be the leader all the time. We should cooperate and help each other.

Finally, I think that sharing everything with God is the most important part of life. Without Him, nothing is possible. This is why I feel my hearing loss will never stop me. No matter what happens to me, I'll never give up.

Thank you, Miss Billington.

The Deaf Actor and Director
Bernard Bragg

National Theatre of the Deaf

BERNARD BRAGG was born in New York City. In 1952, he received his degree from Gallaudet. That fall, he began teaching at the California School for the Deaf in Berkeley. In 1956 he studied with Marcel Marceau in Paris. He received his M.S. at San Francisco State College in 1959. Bernard has worked as a solo mime and had his own television program called "The Quiet Man", a weekly presentation of stories and poems in mime. In 1967 he resigned his teaching position to help found the National Theatre of the Deaf and work as an actor and director.

Mr. Bragg, how did you first become an actor?

As soon as I learned how to lie. I guess that's the way everybody first becomes an actor. "I don't want to go to school today." "I have a headache." You have to be a real good actor to convince your mother!

Then my father had a theatre company, and he put me in plays when I was quite young. Also, I was active in school dramatics. I got leading roles in the plays, partly because my parents are deaf and I was good at signing.

Your parents helped you, didn't they?

They have always encouraged me. They have always enjoyed watching me act. Both are good actors themselves.

What are you doing today?

Besides acting, directing, experimenting, traveling and studying with the National Theatre of the Deaf, I give lectures at schools, colleges and universities. I give drama workshops with hearing students and with deaf students. I teach drama to hearing children in ghetto schools. I teach sign-mime and mime at the NTD summer school. I appear on TV talk shows. I also meet with parents of deaf children, teachers and counselors. I teach mime to interpreters for the deaf. I am doing many things that I have always wanted to do, and am able to do many things that I have never done before.

Looking back, what has helped you reach your goals?

Determination and singleness of purpose. I was not distracted from my goals. People appreciated my efforts and encouraged me. When I was young, the creative process was hard at work in me. I enjoyed things that I created on my own. I immediately lost interest in things that someone forced me to copy.

Can you give an example?

My father gave me Christmas toys every year. The only ones I really liked were a chemistry set and Lincoln Logs. Why? Because I could create things with them. I could build a different house every time I played with Lincoln Logs. My creative drive helped me reach my goals.

**What advice would you give a
deaf youth who wants to be an actor?**

I would say to young people: Look into yourself first, then you will know whether your life belongs to the stage or not. If you know you really belong to the theatre, then study, observe, and work hard. How far you will go depends on your attitudes toward the theatre, toward other people, and most importantly, toward yourself and your art.

There are about eight or ten local theatre groups for the deaf in the United States today. One very good one is the Hughes Memorial Theatre in Washington, D.C. Many schools for the deaf have their own theatre groups. A deaf person wishing to act might start in his school drama club. If he is good enough, he may later perform in Gallaudet or NTD plays.

After college, if he is still interested in acting, he might attend one of the summer workshops NTD holds in Waterford, Connecticut. Outstanding students in these workshops are invited to join NTD.

It's a long road and a hard one. But if a deaf youth really wants to act, he will find a way. I might add that the theatre is much more than just acting. Deaf people can work in lighting, directing, costuming, producing, scenery and many other areas.

What is in the future for you?

I wish the answer were as simple as the question. I will continue experimenting. I hope NTD will grow. I hope that my work, whatever it is, will affect as many people and children, deaf and hearing, as possible. My future lies with NTD because this is where my interest is. My future, like my past, is unpredictable. My life has been exciting and adventuresome. Every opportunity that comes my way changes my life.

Mrs. Helen Powers has written a book about your life and the NTD, published by Dodd, Mead. How do you think the book would help us?

I like to hope the book will help hearing people understand deaf people better, help them see the light and open doors and let deaf children come out freer, happier, better able to communicate . . .

If you had your life to live over, would you do it differently?

The actor in me says yes—the inner me says no.

Thank you Mr. Bragg.

Deaf People and TTY's
Lee Brody

IRWIN LEE BRODY was born in Newark, New Jersey. He attended the Newark School for the Deaf, then went to the Central Institute for the Deaf in St. Louis. He returned to Newark, receiving his high school diploma from Weequahic High School. He graduated from Rutgers University with a degree in Psychology. Today he is self-employed in real estate management and is President of the New York-New Jersey Teletypewriters for the Deaf, Inc.

How did you get interested in TTY's?

One Saturday morning about six years ago, I was on a hunting trip hiking through the woods. I fell on some wet rocks and landed on my back. I was badly hurt and partly paralyzed. I could not get help. I could not call my wife because she is deaf. My children were not home. I was lucky to get home safely by myself, ten hours later.

Two years later, I heard the story of a 38 year-old deaf man's heart attack. His wife tried to get help but couldn't. He died. This story made me see the need for better communications for deaf people. TTY's seemed to be one answer to such life-and-death problems.

Did many deaf people have TTY's at that time?

No. In fact, as late as 1969, only a few deaf people owned TTY's. They were very expensive. Also, few deaf people wanted to spend $350 for one if other deaf people didn't buy TTY's too.

What did you do?

In the spring of 1969, I picked up, repaired and gave about 20 TTY's to my friends, who found them helpful. We set up an organization, the NY-NJ PTTY for the Deaf, Inc. We looked for more TTY's to repair and use.

The Bell Telephone Company helped us set up a training school. Twenty-two deaf friends of mine learned to repair and rebuild TTY's. When they graduated, they became members of the NY-NJ PTTY for the Deaf.

What do these people do?

They build TTY's for sale to other deaf people. When a deaf person buys a TTY, one of our members shows him how to use it. If the machine breaks, we will fix it.

How many deaf people have TTY's now?

In the New York City area, we have about 400 TTY's in use. In the United States as a whole, almost 2,000 deaf families have TTY's. We have a national organization of TTY owners. We are growing fast.

Tell me about your news service.

We have a weekly news service. People call me with their news. Every Friday morning I put the news together. We announce banquets, speeches, marriages, births, funerals and many other things.

In fact, we have news from other areas, including Houston, Texas, Washington, D.C., and Boston, Massachusetts, We hope to have a national news service soon.

What else is new?

We have a new TTY that you can take with you, anywhere you go. It has no motor. It is light and small enough to fit into a briefcase.

Another new TTY hooks onto TV sets. The messages appear on the TV screen. It is called Phone-TV.

A third new machine is a TTY for the deaf-blind. The deaf-blind person can read it by running his hands over the raised print.

Some stores have TTY's now. A deaf person can call the store to buy things. More important, some police stations have TTY's too. Already, lives have been saved.

TTY's are helping deaf people in many ways. At last, we don't have to drive long distances to see if a friend is home. Deaf clubs can advertise their special events. Missing deaf persons can be located with the help of TTY news messages. A lonely deaf person can call friends anywhere in the country.

Most important to me, however, is saving lives. A while ago, for example, I got this call:

> Sue Smith speaking. I wish you to know that TTY has saved my life. I used my TTY to call my deaf friend. She told her hearing mother to call the police. The police got an ambulance to take me to the hospital. Thank you for making TTY possible for the deaf.

It's calls like this that encourage me to work harder.

Thank you, Mr. Brody.

Chance and Choice
Edward Carney

Clif Smith, Jr.

EDWARD CARNEY attended the Virginia School for the Deaf and Pulaski (Va.) High School. Following graduation from Gallaudet, he taught at the Florida School for the Deaf. He has also worked in a manufacturing company, at an aircraft factory, as a rehabilitation counselor and as a program specialist with Media Services and Captioned Films. He is now executive director of the Council of Organizations Serving the Deaf.

How did you happen to have so many jobs?

It was partly chance, partly choice. I quit college when the United States got into World War II. The army wouldn't accept me because of my deafness. But I wanted to serve my country. So I went to Akron to make gun bases. I became "the man behind the man behind the gun."

When the war ended, I taught for two years in Arkansas. Then I decided I should finish college before doing any more teaching.

In those days, people who quit school at Gallaudet usually could not come back. Also, I had a family and married men were not allowed at Gallaudet. So I had to talk my way back. Finally, they accepted me.

I got a full-time job at an ice-cream company. I worked on the night clean-up crew from 4 pm until 1 am every night. I had to be on Kendall Green for classes at 8 in the morning. My wife used to bring the kids to Gallaudet in the afternoon to see Daddy! Finally, I got my B.A. I think I was the first daddy to graduate from Gallaudet!

What did you do then?

I taught for two years in Florida. The school was oral but I wanted to teach in total communication. At the risk of losing my job, I used signs along with speech. The students did very well but the school fired me.

I found a job in a manufacturing company near the school. I kept trying to help the kids, but the school fought my efforts. Two years later, I took my family to St. Louis where I got a job with an aircraft factory. I worked there for nine years. My job was to put bolt A into hole B. It was boring but the pay was good. I had a family to support.

What happened then?

A rehabilitation counselor named Geno Vescovi talked me into working with multiply-handicapped deaf adults in a sheltered workshop in St. Louis. At first, I didn't have the courage to leave my secure job for a new idea that might not work. Geno finally sold me on the idea. We worked very hard on that workshop. It was a real challenge.

From there I moved on to Captioned Films in Washington, D.C.—from choice. This job was another challenge. The program was just starting. I stayed with Captioned Films until I joined the Council of Organizations Serving the Deaf (COSD) as executive director.

What is the COSD?

It is a group of organizations that serve deaf people. The COSD tries to help the organizations work together. We want to improve life for deaf people. We are also interested in an information center on deafness that will help both deaf and hearing people learn more about deafness.

The idea of the COSD is something I really believe in. I think it is important. Deaf people have to work with hearing people, teachers have to work with parents, speech pathologists have to work with rehabilitation counselors. If the COSD can help these people work together, deaf people will benefit.

What have you learned that will help deaf youth?

I have learned that it is important to be flexible, and to have self-confidence. When I began working, I had no master plan, no clear way to go. I had to decide each step of the way where I would go next. Other people often advised me, but the final decisions were mine. This is true of many deaf people. It is sometimes hard to get the job you want. You may have to work in something else until you get your big chance. It takes flexibility. It means you must know when opportunity knocks and be ready to answer. It also means you must be confident and full of a sense of adventure. You must be willing to take some chances if you hope to get your choice.

Thank you, Mr. Carney.

To Be Black and Deaf
Ernest Hairston

ERNEST E. HAIRSTON grew up in West Virginia. After receiving his B.S. from Gallaudet, he taught in North Carolina. Later he became a rehabilitation worker. In 1967 he received his M.A. from California State University at Northridge. Today he works for Media Services and Captioned Films, U.S. Office of Education, in Washington, D.C.

What is it like to be black and deaf?

It's hard sometimes. But most of the time I just accept my blackness and my deafness. Growing up in West Virginia, I began to see that black people are like white people. The only difference is in color. Both blacks and whites have their chances in life.

First I wanted to be a barber. Later, through encouragement, I saw that I could do better than that. So I decided to become a teacher. Being black and deaf made it hard to get a job teaching. Things are better today.

Sometimes being deaf is an advantage. It helped me to go to college. If I were hearing, vocational rehabilitation would not have paid for me to go to Gallaudet. Being black helps sometimes, too. Black deaf professionals are in demand. But you must be able to do the job. Too few black deaf people are ready for these jobs.

To be black and deaf in America today is an advantage for a few. It is very hard for many others.

Is it hard for a deaf black to go to Gallaudet?

Few black deaf persons have gone to college. Andrew Foster was the first. This is changing. More black deaf persons are going to Gallaudet.

Many blacks don't understand why they need a college education. Others think: "I can't do it." They want to work in a factory. They think the factory pays more. It doesn't, in the long run.

We need to help them see why college is important.

Also, black deaf youth don't have enough heroes. Who can they look up to and follow? Where are the successful black deaf people? They need someone to tell them: "You can!"

How can we help them with their problems?

The best way is to bring whites and blacks together. In the West Virginia School for the Deaf, I had two white roommates and one black roommate. We played chess together. We were all on the football and basketball teams. We often played practical jokes on each other. By the end of the year, we were not saying, "those Negro boys with me" or "those white boys." We were "John," "Dick," "Paul," and "Ernie."

What help is needed from vocational rehabilitation?

Black deaf people and their families don't know where to get help. They need guidance.

Also, some rehabilitation counselors don't understand black deaf people. The average black deaf person is under-educated and under-trained. He finds it hard to get services. It is hard for rehabilitation to find him. This all adds up to a big problem.

What can we do?

The biggest need is for black deaf leaders. Black deaf people can help themselves. We need the help of teachers, vocational rehabilitation counselors, employers, and white deaf people.

We must help deaf blacks understand that they *can* be successful. We must help them believe in themselves. A hero, someone to look up to and follow, is important. A black deaf teacher can be a hero to his students. The kids can look at him and say: "If he can do it, so can I."

Thank you, Mr. Hairston.

Dentistry and the Clergy
Edwin Nies

Bárbara Nies

DR. EDWIN W. NIES is a native New Yorker. He became interested in dentistry while at Gallaudet and received his dental training at the University of Pennsylvania. After a long and successful career as a dentist, he became a minister, because he had been active in church activities since college days.

What are you doing these days, Dr. Nies?

I retired from the clergy in 1964. But I'm still busy. I hold two church services each month, in the Diocese of Long Island.

Tell me about your childhood.

I grew up in a clean New York City. Clean streets, electric trolleys and so forth. No pollution then. When I was 6½ years old, I became totally deaf from spinal meningitis. So I attended Lexington School for the Deaf, which was a short walk from my home.

What did you do in your free time?

I continued to play with hearing kids in the area. My father put me to work in a florist shop owned by his friends. The job really made me use my speech and lipreading.

One summer when I was 14 years old, a hearing friend of mine and I had passenger boats for hire. We would row the boats for the passengers. I taught my friend fingerspelling. Later, he was to play an important role in my life.

When I was 16, I went to Gallaudet. I was the youngest student in the preparatory class that year.

How did you get interested in dentistry?

One of my four uncles was a well-known dentist. One day I visited his office. I was very interested in his dental laboratory and learned the work there during summer vacations. After a few summers I knew I wanted to be a dentist.

My uncle never thought a deaf person could become a dentist! I was a little scared too. For me, it was the "impossible dream."

I applied to the University of Pennsylvania. They accepted me. But then, two weeks before school started, they said no—because I was deaf.

What did you do then?

Well, with the help of a hearing friend, I finally convinced the Dean of the Dental Department that I should be given a chance to show that I could do the work.

Was dental school difficult?

Yes, the class was large! For the first time in my life, I couldn't make friends. School was tougher that I had expected. After one month I felt like quitting.

But then I saw a sign: "All Out for Fall Rowing." Oh, boy! I loved rowing. When I went to the river to try out for the team, I saw a boy I knew. He fingerspelled: "I know you!" This was the boy I had taught to fingerspell, eight years before. His name was Frank Zulauf. We were both in the same dental class. From that day on, things got better. Overnight I made new friends. He helped a lot. Without him, I might never have become a dentist.

Did you enjoy being a dentist?

Yes. I had my own office in New York City. I was also dentist to the kids at Lexington School for the Deaf, where I worked two days a week.

How did you get the job at Lexington?

The Superintendent, Dr. Harris Taylor, helped me. Some members of the Lexington School Board of Trustees did not believe I could do it. Dr. Taylor then put his arm around my shoulders and asked the Board to give one of the School's graduates a chance to prove that deafness was not any handicap in professional work. A few years after being appointed to the Lexington staff, I was also appointed to serve the pupils of the New York School for the Deaf (Fanwood).

I hear you served in the war.

Well, not exactly. During World War I, I felt a duty to help my country. But my deafness kept me out of the army. So I served the Family Service Division of the Red Cross as a clinic dentist in NYC for four years.

How did you become a clergyman?

One of my four uncles was a dentist, like I said. Two others were Episcopal ministers. While I was a dentist, I often served at St. Ann's Church for the Deaf, helping out on weekends. For 5 years, they were without a minister. Finally, I was invited to study for the ministry. In 1950 I was ordained a priest and became the Vicar of St. Ann's. While Vicar, I served as chaplain at the Gallaudet Home for the Aged Deaf and for many years have been on the Board of Trustees for the Home. For a while I was also a board member on the Conference of Church Workers Among the Deaf.

Thank you, Dr. Nies.

The Deaf Woman
Nancy Rarus

John Huang

NANCY BLOOM RARUS grew up in New Jersey. After receiving her degree from Gallaudet in 1962, she began teaching at the American School for the Deaf in Connecticut. Ms. Rarus is also very active in the New England deaf community.

Nancy, are you Miss, Ms., or Mrs.?

I'm Ms., thank you.

What does that mean?

Well, if you're not married, you're Miss. If you are married, you're Mrs. But what if I don't want you to know if I'm married or not? I can use Ms. for that. You pronounce it "Mizzz." It is like Mr. for men. Mr. doesn't tell me if you're married or not, does it? So why should I tell you if I'm married or not?

Do you believe in women's lib?

Really, I've always been just myself—a person. That I am a woman is unimportant. I am a person who happens to be female. But I think women's lib has gone too far.

In what way?

The leaders of women's lib want men and women to be equal and the same. They leave nothing to the imagination. I like to keep some imagination. I like to be taken out to dinner, to feel like a woman.

Are many deaf women "liberated"?

More deaf women are independent today. They are more active in the community. But few are active women's libbers.

Maybe you men see now that women can help. This makes you invite them to meetings and conventions. The women become more confident, more sure of themselves. Then they start to do important work.

In the past, the deaf girl was less active. In the school she went along with the rules: time to wake up, time to eat breakfast, time for school, time for play. When she graduated, she got married, had children and brought them up.

Today more deaf women go to college. They see chances to do things in the world. They see that there is more to life than a home and a family.

Today's deaf students—both boys and girls—seem to know more. They are more aware of the world around them. They travel more. They are more sophisticated. I think they will make good leaders.

Do you enjoy teaching them?

Oh, yes. It makes me very happy to see them learn. I also enjoy working with the kids outside the classroom. Teaching is a very rewarding profession for a deaf woman. I just wish more schools would hire deaf teachers. The kids often find that they learn more from a deaf teacher. The communication is easy and we understand each other well.

Your parents are deaf, too. So is your brother. How did you feel at home?

Yes—we are all deaf. But when I left the house I was different. When my deaf friends came to my house, they always had so much fun. It was the signs. We could all understand each other.

Would you like to have normal hearing?

Oh, yes! I know what it is like to be deaf. Now I want to know the other side of the coin—to know what it is like to be hearing. I would like to turn on the radio while I do housework. I'd like to be able to talk well and easily. I'd like a lot of things.

I asked my friends, "Which would you choose—a million dollars or normal hearing?" The older deaf people wanted the money. The younger deaf people preferred to have hearing. Me? I'd take hearing because with it I could earn a million dollars!

Is hearing that important?

To me it is. You see, people want things they can't have. The grass seems greener on the other side of the fence. John Keats, the poet, once said: "Heard melodies are sweet but those unheard are sweeter." I can't have hearing, so I want it.

If you had normal hearing, what would you do?

I'd be an airline stewardess. I know that sounds silly. My friends say a stewardess is just a fancy waitress. But still I'd like to be a stewardess.

If all deaf people suddenly had normal hearing, what would happen?

Oh, wow. That's too unbelievable for words. We'd still get together. Then, maybe we'd have a "Used-to-be-Deaf" Club! It might be harder to go to college without help from vocational rehabilitation, because we would have to pay ourselves, and some of us might not be able to afford it.

What about your children?

I have two—Tim, who is 6 years old and Kim, who is four. They already know that there are deaf people and hearing people. Tim has said twice: "I want to hear." He wants to be a policeman. Sometimes I have to tell him he can't do something because he is deaf.

Isn't that changing?

Yes, it is. Now we have deaf Ph.D.'s. Deaf people are doing all kinds of things. Maybe by the time Tim grows up, there will be deaf policemen. If not, maybe he can be the first.

How did you feel when you first found out that Tim was deaf?

I didn't want to believe it. But later I accepted it. When Kim was born, I expected that she would be deaf too. She is. Sometimes parents are afraid to admit that their child is deaf. They say: "I never thought it would happen to me." Both deaf and hearing parents say this.

Do deaf parents get over the shock faster?

I think so, yes. But it still hurts. Some deaf parents even refuse to allow the child to learn signs. They fear he won't talk. Some "experts" think that deaf parents know all about deafness, that deaf parents don't fear deafness. That's just not true.

There is a lot of misunderstanding about deafness among deaf parents. In fact, I know some deaf people who would want their child to be deaf. Actually want a deaf child because there are so many services. For example, many of us could not have gone to Gallaudet without help from vocational rehabilitation. Today deaf people have a feeling of "oneness"—that other deaf people are their friends. Sometimes being deaf actually helps you get a job.

But this is just part of deafness—the good part. Deafness is so much more than this. To me, deafness is not being able to do what I really want to do.

Thank you, Ms. Rarus.

The Deaf Man at Work
Ben Schowe

Dr. BEN M. SCHOWE lives in Akron, Ohio. For many years he worked for the Firestone Tire and Rubber Company. A Gallaudet graduate, he has written widely about deaf workers in private industry. He was awarded an honorary doctorate from Gallaudet in 1951. Eight years later he retired from his position with Firestone.

How did you become a labor economist?

It was mostly luck. I did not plan it that way. But it was a most unusual opportunity for a deaf man in industrial relations. My only achievement was to take full advantage of the opportunity.

Is it hard for deaf men to get jobs in industry?

The minimum requirements are 1) enough language to understand simple written instructions, and 2) enough arithmetic to make out a time card. These are *minimum* requirements for factory jobs. These requirements are to protect the worker as well as the company.

What do you look for in a worker?

The ability to take hold and push a job through to completion. I never hired a man just because he was deaf or just because he was hearing. I hired him only after I was sure he had this ability. Deaf men with few language skills sometimes did very well on the job. More important than language are "social skills." By social skills I mean the ability to get along with hearing people in the company.

You are called a "maverick." What does this mean?

It means that I do not always run with the crowd. I make my own decisions. I am not afraid to face reality. Often I am the only one who disagrees on popular questions of the day.

Were you always this way?

Not really. A ball game, a skating party, a tennis match—I was in it up to my ears and in spite of my ears. Weak hearing was my problem, but it did not seem to matter to me as a small boy with my friends.

Along the way, I picked up a saying: "To know right from wrong and not to be afraid." This saying was my motto. Then, much later, I discovered that this rule-of-life was not good. There is no "right" or "wrong." Everything is in between.

What are you doing in retirement?

My days are filled with reading and writing. I have played some golf, but have not traveled much. Mostly, I study the problems of deaf people. I think the biggest problem is that the "experts" think they know all the answers. They don't bother to ask deaf people what the real story is.

What is the real story?

Well, one problem is in those bright "success stories" of oral deaf people who lipread and speak perfectly. I'm sure some deaf people can lipread and speak well, but I have never met one who could do it perfectly in every situation. Those extravagant stories make most of us look stupid by comparison. That's not good. When deaf people look for a job, it's hard sometimes because people think all of us should be able to lipread and speak perfectly. But these deaf people do have strength and ability which can be a source of pride to them.

How do you feel about the many services for deaf people today?

I feel some of them are very much needed. But there may be too many services. Deaf people may expect help every time they have a problem. When I was young it was every man for himself. If I had a problem, I had to solve it by myself. That made me work for what I got. When I solved my problems, I was proud. I like deaf people who work out their own problems instead of asking for help all the time.

So what do you live for now?

Discovery. Time spent reading is time filled with the excitement of discovery. For example: if you catch a fish, that's a thrill. But the thrill is gone the next day. But a new idea, a fresh discovery, is a gift from God. It stays with you.

Do you have any new mottos?

One. It is a little poem:

> The wisest thing, I suppose,
>   That a man can do for his land,
> Is the work that lies under his nose,
>   With the tools that lie under his hand.

Thank you, Dr. Schowe.

The Deaf Counselor
Larry Stewart

D<small>R. LARRY STEWART</small> was born in Texas. He received his B.S. from Gallaudet, an M.A. from the University of Missouri, and an Ed. D. from the University of Arizona. Larry has been a teacher, a coach and a counselor. He is now an Associate Professor at the University of Arizona.

Dr. Stewart, what is it like being a counselor?

It is rewarding and interesting. A counselor must be a special kind of friend to his client. The counselor must like the client as a person, really understand the client, and be completely honest. This is asking a lot of the counselor. But this is how he must be if he is to help his clients.

Is it hard to be a counselor if you are deaf?

Sometimes being deaf yourself can make it harder. On the other hand, at times a deaf counselor can help a client in ways that many hearing counselors probably can't. More important than whether you are deaf or hearing, however, is your attitude. If you really want to work with people, you won't let your own deafness stop you.

Can you give us an example of a problem a deaf counselor might have?

Well, suppose you are a counselor and a close friend of a man (Mr. A) who has an enemy in another man (Mr. B). Suppose also that Mr. B knows you are a close friend of Mr. A. Now, if Mr. B has a problem and wishes to have counseling, chances are he will not come to you. He may think you will tell Mr. A about his problem.

Another example is where very close friends of the counselor have marital problems and come to him for counseling. Marital counseling is a difficult business under the best of circumstances. The counselor needs to be objective. As a close friend, he will automatically have personal feelings about the couple. Being human, he may let his feelings confuse his thinking about their marital difficulties.

There are other problems, of course. If the counselor himself has marital problems, people will think he can't give good advice about marriage. If the counselor drinks a lot or argues with others, people will question his ability to counsel.

The truth is that counselors are very human people. They have strengths and weaknesses.

What have you enjoyed most about being a counselor?

The best thing about it has been working with so many different people, seeing them grow and develop and become increasingly responsible for their own lives. I like to see people make something of themselves. When I see them learning to solve their problems, I feel a great deal of satisfaction.

Also, in counseling I have a chance to meet with and work with many people from all walks of life. For me this has been a very rewarding experience. I have worked with farmers, doctors, policemen, judges, public health workers, parents and so on. This has been quite stimulating.

It has been said that people come to know themselves through other people, and I agree.

What would you say to a young deaf person who thought he or she would like to become a counselor with deaf people?

I would not say the same thing to all deaf people.

Perhaps one thing I would say is that the deaf person should try to find out what he really wants. If he or she was sure about wanting to be a counselor, I would ask if he or she understood what counseling is all about. If there were gaps in this knowledge, I would try to help fill the gaps.

I would emphasize that the counselor works with many different kinds of people. These people all have their own values and beliefs. It is not the job of the counselor to tell the client what he should believe. The counselor must let the client be himself. This is not an easy task for the counselor.

I would tell the young deaf person that if he or she really wants to be a good counselor, he should work toward developing a wholesome liking and respect for people, toward understanding how people can solve a wide variety of problems, and toward realizing how to help others learn these problem-solving techniques.

Counseling is not the giving of advice on how to solve problems. Rather it is helping people recognize and deal with problems as part of their development.

The young deaf person would need a master's degree in order to be a truly well-prepared counselor. This degree should be in counseling, in his or her area of interest —school counseling, rehabilitation counseling, mental health counseling, and so forth.

Dr. Stewart, you are an expert on problems of "multiply handicapped" deaf people. Can you tell us about these people?

The words "multiply handicapped" mean that these people have more than one handicap. Deafness is a handicap. If the deaf person is also blind, we say he is multiply handicapped.

Deaf people with other handicaps have many problems. School is often very hard for them. They may find it hard to get a job. Some need special help before they are ready to work. They may need to learn work habits, shop vocabulary, work skills, and living skills. They may also need help in learning to read and write. Many have problems making friends.

What can be done for these people?

Multiply handicapped deaf people can learn. They often need a little more time to learn, but they can become good workers. If we are patient with them and help them grow, I think we may be surprised how well they do. In many ways, multiply handicapped deaf children are like other children. They need to be accepted and loved. They need a chance to decide for themselves what they want in life.

On the other hand, they do have special problems. We need to understand their problems if we are to help them. Most of all, we must accept them as people. If we do that, I think we can do a lot for multiply handicapped deaf people.

Thank you, Dr. Stewart.

The Deaf Man and Insurance
Frank Sullivan

F<small>RANK</small> B. S<small>ULLIVAN</small> was born in Montana. After obtaining his B.A. degree from Gallaudet in 1941, he taught in the South Dakota and West Virginia Schools for the Deaf. Since 1967, he has been Grand President of the National Fraternal Society of the Deaf.

**Mr. Sullivan, is it hard for
deaf people to get life insurance?**

Not as hard today as in the past. Deaf people used to have to pay $5.00 or $10.00 extra each year per $1,000 worth of insurance. Even today, some insurance companies refuse to sell accidental death insurance to deaf people.

What about the National Fraternal Society of the Deaf?

One reason why the NFSD was started was the difficulty deaf people had in getting life insurance at fair rates. The NFSD rates are usually lower than those of other companies.

Is that why you became a member?

More or less, yes. Also, I had strong feelings about the NFSD because it is run by deaf people and they are very proud of their own organization.

Tell me more about your life, Frank.

I was born and raised in Butte, Montana. When I was ten years old I lost my hearing from an attack of spinal meningitis. At that time I was in the fifth grade of a Catholic school. Although I continued going to that school, it was difficult. My habit of reading helped me a lot.

Did you know signs then?

Not at first. Communication with friends was not easy. One day some friends and I saw a picture of the manual alphabet in a dictionary. We learned it. After that, I was happier with my friends. They would also interpret for me in the movies and other places.

During the summer after graduating from the eighth grade and while selling newspapers on the street, I bumped into a blind man. He was angry with me and started yelling at me. I said I could not understand him because I was deaf. He calmed down, started using the manual alphabet and told me about the school for the deaf and the blind. It was only 30 miles away.

So you went to school there?

Yes. The use of signs and fingerspelling, combined with speech and lipreading in the classroom helped a lot. Then I went to Gallaudet. After I graduated in 1941, I became a supervisor of boys at the South Dakota School for the Deaf. A year later I went to the West Virginia School for the Deaf as teacher, coach and supervisor of older boys.

This was during World War II. There were many jobs open, so after working one summer at a good-paying job at Firestone Tire and Rubber Company in Akron, Ohio, I decided to stay there. When the war ended in 1945, I got a job as clerk in the Home Office of the NFSD.

Tell me more about the NFSD.

The NFSD was formed by deaf people themselves, mainly for the reason I explained before. They built it from the ground up. That helps to explain their pride in their Society.

Why do people need insurance?

Because life is very expensive. So is death. If you die, your family needs money to pay for funeral expenses and to help keep them going. If you have an automobile accident, you need money to pay for car repairs. If your house burns down, you need money for a new one. And so forth. The idea behind insurance is to put aside a little money each month or year to protect you when something happens to you, your house or your car. There are many kinds of insurance, but I am mentioning only a few.

How much life insurance must a deaf person buy to become a member of the NFSD?

At least $500. But there is no limit to the amount that you can apply for.

How much would he pay for that $500 worth?

It depends on what kind of insurance he wants and how long he wants to pay on it. The younger he is when he starts paying for it, the less it will cost him.

How big is the NFSD today? How many members?

We are in the best shape ever, with $6,300,000 in assets and close to 13,000 members. Insurance held by these members totals $13,000,000. We have 122 Divisions (lodges) in the U.S. and Canada. Each Division has its own officers. Meetings are held once a month. Our Divisions have projects, like helping aged deaf people, poor and crippled children, and so forth. Our Home Office in Oak Park, Illinois, a suburb of Chicago, has a full time staff of 11 people. In the very near future a new office building will be constructed to take care of our expanding needs.

You have some secrets too, don't you?

Yes. A few mysteries do help draw people in. When they

join, these mysteries are explained to them, like our emblem pin. This pin has a number of symbols on it, each of which has a meaning—the colors, the letters, the geometrical figures.

What do you see in the future?

The NFSD has done a great deal to show the ability of deaf people, and I am sure it will continue to build up an even better image. I have always dreamed that some day every deaf person in America and Canada would be a member of our Society, and this is a good goal to pursue. I love my work, as should anyone who is connected with the movement started by the NFSD.

Thank you, Mr. Sullivan.

Television and Deafness
Jane Norman Wilk

Peter Wechsberg

JANE NORMAN WILK was born and raised in Virginia. She received her B.A. from Gallaudet and M.A. from New York University. After two years with the National Theatre of the Deaf as an actress, she, along with Peter Wechsberg, became newscasters for the deaf with KRON-TV in San Francisco.

Tell me how you became interested in television

Perhaps the word is "why" instead of "how". Peter Wechsberg, my co-newscaster and I discovered that deaf people for the most part meet discrimination every day of their lives. When we were actors with the National Theatre of the Deaf traveling on the road, we saw houses with TV antennas all over the country and realized that television was a means of changing or improving the image of deafness. We then decided to have a news program for the deaf. Once our decision was made, we proceeded to prepare ourselves. Peter went to San Francisco to study filmmaking and I went to New York City to study television. Six months later I joined Peter in San Francisco.

You know, of course, some hearing people have the strangest ideas about deaf people. Perhaps a story could illustrate this point. In my life I have traveled a great deal and have witnessed many situations. One time Peter and I were in a coffee shop talking quite physically, with flying arms and rubber faces. There was this gentleman sitting next to me. After being jabbed in the ribs a couple of times he took out a pen and wrote on the napkin: "Can you read?" and showed me the napkin. I wrote back: "No, but I can write." He read the napkin and I swear to you I saw a tear in his eye. He was very sincere and really believed that I could not read. He did not realize that I would have to be able to read in order to answer his question. I believe this story best explains why I am in television. We are on the air every day. Our program is called NEWSIGN 4. Our purpose is to inform the public.

Was it hard to get the show started?

Yes and no. It was hard to sell the idea to television people but once they understood how many deaf people there were in our area and how important it was to keep deaf people informed, the stations began to open up to the idea of having a news program for the deaf and to the idea of having deaf people on the air. It was a tough and interesting experience which required careful planning and months of deliberations and persistence. We prepared a proposal and went from station to station. KRON-TV 4 was one station that decided to give us a try. We went on for thirteen weeks to see how the general public would respond. After thirteen weeks we signed a contract with KRON-TV 4. Response was fantastic and we had articles about our program in nationwide magazines such as NEWSWEEK and TV GUIDE plus articles in major publications of the deaf. We are now in our second year.

What is your day like?

Wake up at five, arrive at the station at 6:30 A.M., along with Peter, Kit and Stephanie Corson (our voice-over narrators who read the news simultaneously). We compile some of the news and our producer compiles other news. Then we pool our efforts along with special-interest news about the deaf. We then interpret and translate the news in Ameslan. Then we go downstairs to the studio, put on makeup and run through to time our news delivery. Then exactly at 8:25 A.M. we are on the air. Afterwards, we watch the playback tape of our program and take down notes and criticisms. Then we go to our office where we begin another day of writing letters, seeing people and preparing future programs for the deaf. We also serve as an informal referral agency.

Is NEWSIGN 4 helping to change the image of deafness?

Definitely yes. There is no question in my mind. A story could best illustrate how effective our purpose is. There is this one deaf woman who worked in a place for ten years. She had never communicated with her fellow workers.

One day she became very ill and could not work. She used up all of her sick leave and annual leave. Finally she recovered and returned to work knowing that she would not get money for the time she was out from work. When she arrived her supervisor handed her a check in full for the whole time she was absent from work. Surprised, she asked her supervisor: "How come?" Her supervisor explained that they had watched NEWSIGN 4 and realized that she was just as human as they. So now, after ten years of working with these people and not communicating with them, she is teaching them signs. If this can happen here in San Francisco, think what can happen all over the country. People here in San Francisco have a completely different concept of deafness. Job opportunities have occurred and we have found jobs for several deaf people. Discrimination against the deaf has lessened. As for the deaf viewers, they are much more interested in what is happening in this everchanging world of ours.

Have you learned anything that would help younger deaf people?

If there is anything I can share with the deaf kids of America, this would be it: don't let anybody tear down your self-image. Self-image is the way you see yourself or how you think of yourself. Do not let anyone tear down or destroy what you think of yourself. Our world is small and the numbers of deaf people are small. We can be hurt by gossip and tearing each other down. Remember, when you tear down another deaf person, you also tear yourself down. We must help other deaf people to help themselves. Support your deaf friends. You will see that you will be paid back for your help. You are the most important person in the world . . . important enough to help yourself, and important enough to help each other.

Thank you, Ms. Wilk.

Wrestling in Arkansas
Nathan Zimble

NATHAN ZIMBLE was born in Massachusetts. At Gallaudet he became an outstanding wrestler. Later, as a teacher and principal at the Arkansas School for the Deaf, he coached many championship wrestling teams. In 1969 he was elected to the American Athletic Association of the Deaf Hall of Fame.

How did you lose your hearing?

I was 14 years old when I got sick with spinal meningitis. I was in the hospital for more than a year. First I lost my sight, then the sight came back again. Then I became deaf. But I did not know it. I thought the hospital was just quiet. After all, they *did* have a sign saying "Hospital Zone—Quiet."

Did you know any deaf people then?

No. I knew nothing about deafness. I went home. My uncle took me to many doctors. Finally he sent me to the Horace Mann School for the Deaf—an oral school. I was there for three months.

Did you like it there?

No. I could lipread but they forced me to take lipreading lessons. I could talk but they forced me to take speech lessons. My mother then put me in the Pennsylvania School for the Deaf in Mt. Airy. Again, they tried to teach me to talk. I kept running home. Mother kept bringing me back. One day the Headmaster, a kind man named Dr. Crouter, told me about Gallaudet College.

So you went to Gallaudet?

Yes. I was very thin and very small. I weighed 100 pounds. My step-brother went to Gallaudet with me to take care of me. He carried the suitcase in one hand and pulled me with the other hand. We went into College Hall. There was a big line. We stood in the line. Soon we came to the registration room. Professor Hughes, the great football coach who was deaf himself, looked at me. He thought I was a grammar school student. He sent me and my brother to Kendall School. It was nearby. Kendall School is a school for the deaf—not a college.

You were small and 15 years old, right?

Yes. Mr. Roberts was at Kendall. He asked my name. Seeing no Zimble on the list of names, he asked me: "Are you sure you should be in Kendall?" I said, "No, I want to go to Gallaudet." They sent me back to College Hall. Hughes was still there. He sent me back to Kendall. To be sure we got there, he sent a Gallaudet student with us. When we got to Kendall, I showed my card to Mr. Roberts. The card said I was a student at Gallaudet. So he told me to show the card to Professor Hughes. Back to College Hall again. When Hughes saw the card, he said: "Oh boy! That's the kind of football material they're sending me now!"

Well, you made it to Gallaudet.

Yes. I had some trouble there. You see, I did not know signs. In my junior year, I had a course in Public Speaking. I thought I'd fail because of my signs. I was surprised to find that I knew more signs than I thought. So I passed the course. From that time on, I learned many signs.

How did you start wrestling?

Well, I was so small that other students would toss me around. They would throw me around like a volleyball. I didn't like that. One day my friend Uriel Jones suggested I learn to wrestle. So I began practicing every day. I practiced with boys from Kendall. There was no one my size at Gallaudet! I practiced for two years. At last, I was good enough. The boys at Gallaudet stopped pushing me around. I was strong enough to fight back.

How did you get on the wrestling team?

Just for fun, they put me on the team one year. I beat boys from other colleges. They usually weighed more than I did, but I won. In fact, I won the 112-lb. Middle Atlantic Championship. It was then that they started calling me Mighty Atom! After that, I tried out for the Olympics. I won second place there, but did not go to the Olympics. That was the end of my college career on the mats.

What happened in Little Rock?

I went to the Arkansas School for the Deaf to teach. I saw many boys who had nothing to do. They were too small for the big sports. So we started a wrestling program. We started with twelve kids. A few days later, 40 kids showed up. I could not teach that many boys. But they were interested. I told them to find shorts—we called them trunks. They did—they cut off their school band slacks above the knee to make shorts!

Did they get into trouble for that?

Well, the band teacher was furious. But the Superintendent said: "If they are smart enough to find a way to join the team, we can't punish them." So they joined the team. The first year the team won some matches. After that first year, we won the state championship for thirteen years straight! I was named "Man of the Week in Arkansas Sports." I also served eight years as the chairman of the State AAU (American Athletic Union) committee on wrestling. I was the only deaf man on the committee.

Later you moved to Philadelphia, right?

Yes. I was working as a watch repairman. But I had to give that up when my eyes became weak. My brother-in-law got me a job with the Mushroom Transportation Company, where I still work. A few years ago, I took a leave of absence to teach math in the Rome (New York) School for the Deaf. I taught there for one year, then came back to Mushroom.

You are famous for your loud voice. How did you get it?

Before I lost my hearing I had a very high voice. In fact, I used to sing in the glee club. At Gallaudet, sometimes I sang just before going to sleep. One night a teacher heard me singing. He thought someone was sick and groaning! More recently, I called my next door neighbor on the phone—talking into it. I told him I wanted to play cards with him. Halfway through the call, I saw our doorbell lights flashing. I turned around to see my neighbor at the foot of the stairs. He said: "Put that phone down. I heard you through the window!"

Anyway, I got in the habit of talking loudly when I was teaching in Arkansas. Some of my students were hard-of-hearing. There were no hearing aids in those days. So I talked very loudly so they could hear me. The teachers in the other building said I was so loud they could set their clocks by my voice! Almost the same thing happened in the Mushroom company recently. The boss is always telling me to keep my voice down. One day, he walked in and asked me to read a message out loud. I thought it was strange but I read it. Then I asked why. He told me: "Our intercom just broke down!"

What do you do in your spare time?

We have an organization called the Delaware Valley Coordinating Services for the Deaf. Deaf people come to us with problems. We try to help them. I was the first director of the organization's adult education program. We held classes in the Mt. Airy School. Deaf people themselves chose the subjects—language, math, current events. We had lectures on insurance, filling out tax forms and so forth. My wife taught classes in language. We also taught sign language to hearing people, parents of deaf children and teachers of the deaf. Then we set up the Delaware Valley Tele-Communications for the Deaf. I am Vice-President. We help get people TTY's. I also took part in the meetings of parents who wanted Total Communication at Mt. Airy. Mt. Airy recently started using Total Communication in the middle and upper schools. The teachers are learning to communicate. Good!

Thank you, Mr. Zimble.